And Her Soul Out Of Nothing

The Brittingham Prize in Poetry

The University of Wisconsin Press Poetry Series
Ronald Wallace, General Editor

Places/Everyone • Jim Daniels
C. K. Williams, Judge, 1985

Talking to Strangers • Patricia Dobler
Maxine Kumin, Judge, 1986

Saving the Young Men of Vienna • David Kirby
Mona Van Duyn, Judge, 1987

Pocket Sundial • Lisa Zeidner
Charles Wright, Judge, 1988

Slow Joy • Stefanie Marlis
Gerald Stern, Judge, 1989

Level Green • Judith Vollmer
Mary Oliver, Judge, 1990

Salt • Renée Ashley
Donald Finkel, Judge, 1991

Sweet Ruin • Tony Hoagland
Donald Justice, Judge, 1992

The Red Virgin: A Poem of Simone Weil • Stephanie Strickland
Lisel Mueller, Judge, 1993

The Unbeliever • Lisa Lewis
Henry Taylor, Judge, 1994

Old & New Testaments • Lynn Powell
Carolyn Kizer, Judge, 1995

Brief Landing on the Earth's Surface • Juanita Brunk
Philip Levine, Judge, 1996

And Her Soul Out Of Nothing • Olena Kalytiak Davis
Rita Dove, Judge, 1997

And Her Soul Out Of Nothing

Olena Kalytiak Davis

The University of Wisconsin Press

The University of Wisconsin Press
1930 Monroe Street
Madison, Wisconsin 53711

3 Henrietta Street
London WC2E 8LU, England

8   7   6   5   4   3

Printed in the United States of America

Cover photograph, *Nude, 1936*. Photograph by Edward Weston,
copyright © 1981 Center for Creative Photography, Arizona Board
of Regents.

Library of Congress Cataloging-in-Publication-Data
Davis, Olena Kalytiak.
   And her soul out of nothing / Olena Kalytiak Davis
      106 pp.   cm.—(The Brittingham prize in poetry)
ISBN 0-299-15710-5 (cloth: alk. paper).
ISBN 0-299-15714-8 (pbk: alk.paper)
I. Title. II. Series
PS3554.A93757A8 1997
811'.54—dc21   97–15599

Halyna Bartkiw Kalytiak (1929–1985)

Roman Michael Kalytiak (1922–1996)

Somebody once said to me,

"We must make the same efforts as lost, desperate beings."

believe me, with a handshake,

Vincent

Contents

Acknowledgments

Grateful acknowledgment is made to the editors of those publications in which the
following poems originally appeared:

Agni: "Perhaps By Then You Will No Longer Be In Love"; "The Unhoused Heart"
The American Voice: "Your TV Lit You Like A Roman Candle"
Ascent: "Father's Famous Devastation"
Countermeasures: "Resolutions In A Parked Car"
Exquisite Corpse: "The Panic Of Birds"
Field: "It Was A Coffin That Sang"; "I've Always Been One To Delight In The Misfor-
    tunes Of Others"
Fine Madness: "The Outline I Inhabit"; "Hey Precious, Listen"; "An Imaginative
    Study In Degradation"
Indiana Review: "There May Be More Of This World Than Can Possibly Exist"; "A
    Few Words For The Visitor In The Parlor"
The Journal: "Another Underwater Conversation"; "Against Devotion"
The Kenyon Review: "In Defense of Marriage"; "As Empty As A Church, I Believe I
    Am A Small Testament To The Failing Relationship Between Space And Light"
Michigan Quarterly Review: "Thirty Years Rising"
New England Review: "Palimpsest"; "Like Working At Wal-Mart"
North American Review: "All The Natural Movements Of The Soul"
Northwest Review: "It's Shaped Like A Fork"; "Angels And Moths"
Permafrost: "Ovarian Tree"
Poet Lore: "Buhrstone"
Poetry Northwest: "Like Kerosene"
Sojourner: "Should One Prefer Purity To Intensity Of Soul?"
We Alaskans: "A Seasonal Dwelling"; "The River Twists Like Lake Shore Drive";
    "Postcard"; "Moorer Denies Holyfield In Twelve"

"Thirty Years Rising" was reprinted in *Best American Poetry 1995*.
"A Few Words For The Visitor In The Parlor" was reprinted in *New American Zeen*.

Thanks to The Rona Jaffe Foundation, the Alaska State Council on the Arts, and
the Juneau Arts and Humanities Council.

Special thanks to Mark Cox, David Rivard, Dean Young, and Mary Ruefle. Some of these poems belong to them.

"I'm Only Now Beginning To Answer Your Letter" is for my friend Tim Shea.

Thank you, Jim Davis. You helped most.

A Few Words For The Visitor In The Parlor

Every time you wish the sky was something happening to your heart, you lose twice.

Mother kept sending me back to the kiosk. Where they wrapped the paper in fish. Pivovarov and the other artists, they were worried. The blood was Ukrainian and it was all over the place. *Go and wash your face.* No, no one said anything about auto-workers. I am simply saying to you what my mother said. I am simply saying what Pivovarov painted: *Go and wash your face. People are coming soon. It is not good for them to see you looking like this.*

I slept the afternoon, but you know what Breton says: I was not in the mood for visitors. Picture yourself inside that word. And yes, my house is a word, but my words, aren't they words also? Today, the sky just wouldn't happen. Today, I was blind sided. Neither pain, nor its powdered absence. Like most days, I became the kitchen sill. I'm simply saying what I always say: what is lace-winged cannot be strong.

My wedding dress hangs at the end of things. It's the kind of thing you think while sitting on someone else's couch: *There is something elegant implied by length.* Or: *So this is a living room, what was I thinking.* Grass stains where the peach-colored silk drank in the ground. But when I get home the urge to clean immediately leaves me. Alone, I can only think of visiting those plain and exotic places. Oh, my cloud covered heart.

She was a branch covered in hoarfrost. I must forgive myself. Something clings to the whore's hem. Dear visitor: you divide your age in two then square it by a dying mother. I am always gathering her up in my arms. Believe me, you never forget someone that thin. You start remembering the way that summer lay differently on top of that year. The hood burns you. I tried driving as gently as I could, but you know, the road had last winter inside it, the winter before. That drive was painful, just look at her face. You remember because someone starts talking about time. Someone says *time, time is like water.* Someone says: *There was once a living room made entirely of death.*

Today, the sky was white. And the ground was white, too. Yet, I could tell them apart. They were that easy to distinguish.

I'm Only Now Beginning To Answer Your Letter

Remind me of your affliction.

I'd like a chronological exhibit
of the disorders leading up to our
conversation, like your old driver's licenses
arranged in that one thin pocket of leather,
the phases of your hair, the splay
of your youth. Your current
eyes distorted by lenses, you're speaking clearly,
louder than the drugs prescribed.

What I want to know about is the frenzy.

Sure, I can picture you
on Christmas Eve needing Mass
to last as long as a bottle of wine, but
I don't get the religion.

Explain Jesus.

Talking with you was like opening an empty drawer.

Talking with you was like emptying an open drawer.
My hands overflowing with garments out-dated, or never worn.
What do you call that thing a priest wears
around his neck? The scarf of a priest . . .

Explain how we're so immediately alive.

And how far can I carry the thought of you
when already the snow won't hold me.
Even rosaries get tired.

And you're not thinking me,
you're just imagining my dead sisters.

You say you want to feel
the words.

You just want to live in Boston
with the painter Martha McCollough.

Sure, I can imagine the thought
of an easel, the idea
of thick paint.

But I want you to explain it simply, clinically.

Because now that I've thought about it, what
doesn't begin with love and death and end
in loneliness?

I'm only now beginning to answer your letter:
Remind me of your affliction.

Like Working At Wal Mart

She heard sad things all day
long in the usual turning
of phrases until it felt
everything she was touching
was just a neatly packaged beauty
supply or a deeply discounted
drug; what everyone needed: detergents
and cosmetics; she scanned shells
for shotguns and rounds for 22s;
and while handling cheap bras and polyester
socks she began to feel the flimsiness
of the lives of others.

That grasping suddenly altered her
thinness into transparency,
and their eyes took turns clutching her
to glean the shape of her bones.
Then they could offer their own
thorns: One had a stray wife who was still
beautiful. Another a faithful wife
with eyebrows as dark as hers, also still,
also beautiful, but betrayed. Finally,
a pregnant wife. We're all older now,
only smoking once a week and it has
something to do with religion. With a world
you can no longer fist. With a wife.

No one she knows has killed himself,
yet. The fat guy at the gas station
thinks of her daily and she remembers:
outside the church it's the day she married
and this perfect stranger comes up to her
and says: Now what do I do
with the rest of my life?

Another Underwater Conversation

It's dangerous, because the brain
sits right next to the ears. I remember
being infected in a suddenly flooded Paris,
my ugly American brain boiled in a french
sea; but such stunning drug induced dreams:
I swam in black and white Chanel, mouthed
perfect verbs, sent pluperfectly sound bubbles
up for air. The fear of conjugation

no longer holding me under the present tense.
On Friday, the dinner conversation moves
from france to work to the other tree
in the Garden of Eden and the next thing you know
Julie's saying the last time she had sex
was three years ago with this guy
she was engaged to marry. He's about to tell her
he's gay. Then Jim starts explaining the thin
glass of friendship, but mostly, I think
he's talking about his childhood dog.
Sometimes, I can listen without lifting a hand

to the voice of desperation speaking
after the beep. Sometimes, I don't offer
a thing. I'm screening everything because that could be me
calling home after struggling to remember the number,
that might be me caught without luck, burning
in the blazing heat reflected off a tar black road,
the taste of bitumen on my sleeve. I can't imagine what

I've called to say. It's not an aria.
No one's singing the facts. But I listen to myself
for hours: trying not to sound desperate, but beginning to
repeat things, because that's how important
things are starting to seem. Sometimes, you call up

your own aphasia. You turn
your good ear. Sometimes, you don't want to hear
the way he fucked her before calling
the whole thing off, oh, the replay, the revival,
the message on the answering machine, your father
whispering after the funeral: now I'm the father
and the mother. It all starts to sound the same.
It's all french. What have you stolen?
What are you giving back?

But, It's Jazz

He's doing his best
Dexter Gordon, he scratches
it out of his throat: "Music,"
in a ragged whisper
"is my life."
Like a man on horse
he hears the galloping inside him,
turns it up louder,
he's found his crazy rhythm, but she,
she needs a refill on her pain
or a compress to lay on her panic.
She imitates that soprano sax
until she is as mad as that one note
that freezes, but refuses to hang
from the trees.

The Way He Sold It

Billy Jones goes and hangs himself
from a telephone pole

up on 6th

like he's ringing somebody up

like he doesn't want to find himself entangled

in the new mess of morning light
the suicide note says
Fuckers wouldn't let me marry my wife

now the fuckers can't find any next of kin
now the fuckers are saying he died stinking drunk

fuckers hated Billy Jones
the way he asked for it
the way he sold it
the way he wore that fox head
on top of his own

now the fuckers are digging a grave in the fog
now the fuckers are standing all between all those crazy
arms of crosses

now the fuckers gently bury him

The Weathered Houses On Ptarmigan Road

Drunk or dead or lucky,
you choose, you decide
in which part of town to settle.
Loose sunlight, a white momentarily suspended, spills
over baked houses, wood weathered
the color of rust or sand,
on crutches, held up above the muck.
And the neighbors are drinking,
thinking: soon someone will have to get up,
go out for cigarettes and eggs
to fry up for the kids who are
also dissolving
into a different tense,
the one that you use to speak of the past
as the future, the one that holds
the simple vocabulary of my own fenced-in childhood:
tame ants crawling on domestic peonies, a clean solid swing.
Even there I worried, dreamt of a mother who impersonated
my mother, looked just like her but drank,
pushing the iron or the vacuum with her free hand.
Even today I'm walking this road of ice
to find the children who want to lick
the walls, taste something as sweet
as a finger dipped in icing, not Gordon's
and Bud whitewashing the walls, making
everything too sunny, too bright,
as their mother opens her mouth wide,
swallows, and sound goes down
then reaches up and out in a guttural
language, ancient, but still
spoken here, shouted above the TV, a language
of long words that are really small ones
sewn together like pelts.
The neighbors drinking, thinking slowly,
betting on when the river will break,
wash away empty bottles and cartons, and

their children, who are—Wait—yes,
still outside, under that young strong star
refusing to go down, thinking
they can go on this way forever,
in this longspun day that pools,
moves mud, takes nothing more important
than it gives away. They'll play this way
forever because this day won't
end, it stretches out, the backyard's
fenceless, a tundra,
they're not even hungry,
they'll never have to go back inside,
they'll never have to breathe
that other air, filter it through their dull
colored bedsheets. They'll never again dream
of that other mother
who smells like cherry Pop-Tarts
toasting, not yet burnt.

Father's Famous Devastation

Father was a Swedenborgian, but he kept his sense
of humor. Taught us that what mattered

was contained in just another pleasant afternoon
near Windsor Park, the stewed rabbit gently seared
and swallowed. In the summer sky a brown thrasher,
a tussock moth in the summer trees, and his two sons.

But the Swedenborgian truth of the matter
is that it's about to hit. I'm just letting him
sit there a while longer, but we all know
what's going to happen: first that vague something

settling just above his eyes, like a brown thrasher,
a tussock moth, but on the inside of his head.
Let's let him loosen his tie, but there's something
not quite right about his fingers, the knot

in his tie, his waistcoat, why is he wearing it?
And it comes over him, it descends
and the afternoon doesn't exist, only the nausea

of nothing
as he almost raises his hands to stop it.

And his sons, and his daughter, and his wife.

He will not get over this for months. He will suffer
a periodic recurrence for the rest of his life.
Henry and I will try not to mention it in our letters.
Instead, I will offer: "the soul is merely the sum
of our mental life." And he will answer,
"you could be right."

Who Cares About Aperture

She may be a lover, may not.
It's like walking into a church.
Who cares about aperture, about crawlspace?
I sat on the front steps with my arms
turned up. Such a small bird with such a long beak.
As if that wasn't my life behind me, inside that house.
As if those logs were something other
than trees. The thing is, he kept saying, in the summer
all you want to do is fish. She may be a lover, may not.
It's like walking into a church.
I sat on the front steps with my arms
turned up. Who cares about aperture,
about crawlspace? As if that wasn't my life. Such a small bird
with such a long beak. Behind me, inside that house.
The thing is, he kept saying, in the summer
all you want to do is fish. As if those logs
were something other than trees. She may be
a lover, may not. It's like walking
into a church. Inside that house. Who cares
about aperture, about crawlspace?
Such a small bird with such a long beak.
The thing is, he kept saying, in the summer
all you want to do is fish.

When it's this windy doesn't it seem impossible
to grow old?

The Outline I Inhabit

1. *Imagine What Pain Says*

In the ghost-making fog the phone rings.

Sure, I'm unnerved, but I listen.
I strain for meaning. So when I hang up
everything's sore. When I hang up
I have to write down everything
that hurts.

Imagine what Pain says:
I'll keep in touch.

2. *The Entire Nonexistent Conversation*

In the ghost-making fog I lose the outline
I inhabit so well. I get so stoned
I have to sit with my imaginary head
between my fantastic knees. I get so stoned
I get so stoned I forget the entire
nonexistent conversation.

3. *The Entire Nonexistent Conversation*

Did I tell you I think I'm in love
with a certain type of cloud? Did I tell you
that now I'm dreaming solely
in Yup'ik? Did I mention which syllables
I'm starting to distort?

4. *A Dull Hum*

It must have been too much.
I must have blown an ear-drum.
Because first there was all that dreadful
music and now there's nothing,
a dull hum.

My brain sounds
just like an old refrigerator.
First, all that vibrating.

Now, a lone drone
on the left.

5. *Not Delineating*

Walking down Chief Eddie Hoffman Highway.

I'm not thinking about composition.
I'm not delineating anything.

6. *De-Composing*

Walking down Chief Eddie Hoffman Highway.

I'm feeling terrifically heavy.
I'm feeling as well grounded as the dead.

Something More Fragile Than This

Quick,
before our bodies turn themselves in,
with a reverence reserved for the dead touch me
because I want to remember how beautiful I still am.
While Spring snows around us, cracking her eggs
on our windows, in her meager dress of yellowing-white,
because I want to rise into today.

So why the urge to render something
more fragile than this?
Why, always, the soul blowing glass?
The soul, once again, filling the lungs
with smoke because a memory of regret sweats
in the plastic sleeve of a family
album. Because there's a snapshot caught
between the pages of some thick book:
my heavy 20 year old frame setting off
the 60lb weight of a dying mother. Because
somewhere, there's a negative slide
of my heart. Because and because and because
I'm sure there's a photo
in some drawer that shows me dressed in black.

But I want to devote myself to the mystery
of this afternoon. I want to honor this
falling night, worship the hour vanishing
between six and seven. This moment
where I'm standing against myself and against
you with a taste in my mouth
that's yolk.

With Bob Marley taking that one long drag
on the refrigerator door.

With the smell of spring.

Moorer Denies Holyfield In Twelve

Caesar's Palace.
The way life keeps splitting itself in two.

Twenty four hours later Florida
had pushed itself under
the wheels of our white Olds.
My father getting out
of the car. I'm squinting, his
shirt is that bright.

I was stunned for a minute
but was able to clear my head.

I'm on the phone now, trying to keep this front
from moving over his white cloud of a head,
because my father used to be two men,
but now he's old.

One minute you're talking weather. Then,
a nasty left-right in the second round.

I didn't mean to start talking obstacles, hooks,
comebacks.
But, suddenly, I'm going down, saying:

I've been holding on with my teeth.
I've developed this strange social stutter.

I had to let my cutman go.

To Those Capable Of Deriving The Greatest Benefit

Let's sort the injury from the injured,
Asking: What field? What battle?

Is this the site of your disaster?

An emergency room full of old friends.
Someone asking: Recollect, if you will,
A poem of Pindar's: *That which above all*

Shines through everything. Shines through
Each thing present all around.

Everything quietly unconcealing in the golden hospital
Light. Here's the chart, the anamnesis, of how and when
We want to kill each other, let each other die.

We, the living, breathe
Although we have lost old friends.

We have left them behind like dirty bandages.
We have left them ripped open, wide.
We've left rooms saying: Fuck you
And you and you.

Saying: Recollect, if you will . . .

Everyone quietly decomposing under the golden
Hospital light. Saying: *That which shines through* . . .

Saying: Let strophe equal antistrophe.

We, the breathing, live
Although we've lost limbs and brain stems,

Let us now sort the injured from the injury . . .

Resolutions In A Parked Car

After I'm done pleading with the steering wheel,
after I'm done screaming at the white doors
of the Friendship Inn, no, even while I'm spitting

and howling, I know, yes, this is the way
we find out about ourselves: crying in rental cars
in parking lots in strange cities that are already

too familiar. The huge ship in front of you,
don't you hope it will soon disembark? Don't you
hate hotels? Don't you hate to travel

just to see the same old pockmarks and limps,
the weight carried below the waist
and above? Just look at what we have done

to ourselves, and topped it off with a club sandwich,
a scribble of neon. I'm wailing
like some foreigner in a foreign country

we don't give a shit about because how could we
understand something as subtle as the mutilation
of ears and lips? Please, I beg you,

perform some crazy rite over me so things can either
finally dissolve or finally become solid.
Please, I need something primitive and complex

to relieve me of this world subdivided into better
and better ways to avoid life. Sicker
and sicker ways. Someone is brewing

their own beer. Someone knows why he is
the best candidate for the job. Death cruising
down 90. Laughing. Sweetheart, Death is the least of it.

I'm in a parking lot in Spokane reintroducing myself
to myself. I'm feeling like throwing up.
In a parking lot in Spokane I am resolving

to read Nietzsche, to pierce and tattoo myself,
in a parking lot I'm determining things
about my labia and nose and heart.

Mutilated Versions Of My Personality Write Poems, Treat Me With Irony And Condescension

And another morning wasted.

Another morning bent over Pessoa's crazy catafalque,
looking for the
sky.

You know to me, Fernando, *catafalque* always sounded
like a dirty word. Sure, I had heard,
had understood the warnings:
Soon we would all be dead.

But *soon? Soon* was a fermata.

You could sing *soon*, but you couldn't mean it.
And then, *soon* grew wings.

Soon was a bird. A sad one. And another

morning wasted
on these subtle griefs:

Each new *loneliness* needed a streetname.
Each pedestrian out on Rua dos Douradores a *soul*.

Maybe in the movie version Sean Penn could play Pessoa.
Sean Penn, somebody troubled.
Maybe in the movie version, the director will get it all wrong.

Is this where the poem turns
discursive? Is this where the poem refers
to its own unmaking?

PROP. XX. The more every man endeavors, and is able to seek what is useful to him—in other words, to preserve his own being—the more is he endowed with virtue; on the contrary, in proportion as a man neglects to seek what is useful to him, that is, to preserve his own being, he is wanting in power.

In other words, this is where you carefully put the Spinoza
down.

And you find a scrap
of paper on your desk that simply says: LUCK.

This is the part of the day where you finally get dressed.

And soon he will come home and ask you: *What did you do all day?*
and you'll say it:

Nothing.

(There's a detachment over there in that arctic meadow.
But that solitude, that isn't yours.)

You'll *say*:

All morning I watched the *sky*
from a place where I couldn't see it.

I mourned something all day long.

But it was *nothing*. I was *nothing*.
All day just *was*.

Here's where you're allowed to go back
to your own, your own,
you know,

loneliness.

LUCK.

Nothing.

I've heard nothing cry.

Cry like a bird?

A loon? Was it a loon?
A sad one?

It's ok, that bird should remind you of something.
Something *troubled*.

And a voice will say: Don't you worry.

A voice (maybe Sean Penn's) will say: *Soon,*
soon we will all be dead.

And, Pessoa? Pessoa sat

alone, at a crowded table
in the middle of a cafe
in the middle of a LISBON.

Pessoa was simply asking for aspirin
and truth. Sometimes it helps
to know someone has already thought
what you are thinking. *Sometimes it doesn't.*

Sometimes it makes it worse. You're thinking
you're *catafalqued*. You're thinking you
have only one or two options:

You can gather the shards of your mirror and walk
through fields and fields heavy, stubbled
with stars, toward the frozen river. Or you can wait here

for the chorus of young women
to carry your voice down
from that mountain
which is already beginning to cover
and recover in clouds
and in snow.

The Scaffolding Inside You

Your thoughts have hung themselves from nails
like workshirts.

The sky has stopped
offering you reasons to live and your heart is the rock
you threw through each window
of what's deserted you, so you turn
to the burnt out building inside you: the scaffolding
overhead, the fallen beams,
the unsound framework;

according to the blue that's printed on the inside of your arms
you have no plans, no plans
uncovered, or uncovering: the offing is emptying,

the horizon empty

now that your sanity is
a tarp or a bedsheet
in the rough hands of the wind,

now that everything is hooded
in drop cloth.

It didn't happen
overnight. Or maybe it did:

your heart, the rock;
your soul, the Gothic barn.

You've even started envying the flowers their stems.

Will the Norther let up?

Will the moon ever again be so full of itself
that that ragged barn will fill with light, through its tin-covered roof?

You should bury more than the dead.
You should try harder.
You should give up.

The Panic Of Birds

The moon is sick
Of pulling at the river, and the river
Fed up with swallowing the rain,
So, in my lukewarm coffee, in the bathroom
Mirror, there's a restlessness
As black as a raven
Landing heavily on the quiet lines of this house.
Again, the sun takes cover
And the morning is dead
Tired of itself, already, it's pelting and windy
As I lean into the pane
That proves this world is a cold smooth place.

Wind against window—let the words fight it out—
As I try to remember: What is it
That's so late in coming? What was it
I understood so well last night, so well it kissed me,
Sweetly, on the forehead?

Wind against window and my late flowering brain,
Heavy, gone to seed. Pacing
From room to room and in each window
A different version of a framed woman
Unable to rest, set against a sky
Full of beating wings and abandoned
Directions. Her five chambered heart
Filling with the panic of birds, asking: What?
What if not this?

Hey Precious, Listen

Now that my heart has stopped
screaming it is just a tired ambulance
parked on the left side
of a highway six lanes thick.

The driver is thinking.
The driver thinks tragedy is a joke.
He thinks: No accident, this.
He starts thinking about a place
where wingspan is not
a flip of a coin,
where birds pass themselves
off as doorbells,
where you don't have to choose
between calamity
and light.

Thirty Years Rising

I needed to point to the buildings, as if they all stood
for something, as if Detroit could rise again
into its own skyline, filled in
as it always is inside me:
each cracked sidewalk, each
of the uniformed girls, braided
and quiet as weeds, each bicycled boy, each man
with a car and a wife, the ones I slept with
and arranged, neatly, like a newly laid
subdivision.

But I was driving with my brother
who doesn't like to think
of the thirty years rising
inside us, the leavened truth. He's arrived
at the heavy black X of destination
on the inside of his forehead
and he doesn't want to see me
looking like this: open-palmed
and childishly dressed, with hipbones
instead of children, aching
to put my sneakered feet on his new leather
dash.

He doesn't want to hear me
say something fucked-up, something like:
It's in my bones. My sternum
runs like Woodward Avenue,
it's pinnated, parked on, full
of dirt, holding women in wigs and cigarettes, bars
lit from the outside in, it's overflowing
with pooltables and ashtrays. My ribs
are holding up factories and breweries, two-bedroom
houses and multi-storied lives, this strip,
this city, these sidestreets,
a bony feather.

He's lived here all his life.
But I gave up these streets
for so many others. I hopped
turnstiles to ride the Metro,
memorized EL tracks and Muni stations
until I had a huge worn subway
map on the inside of my head, but couldn't get off at any stop,
couldn't begin to live in any city, and couldn't sleep
with anybody but myself. I gave up
this body for so many others. I've been both
an exaggeration of myself and someone
who looks just like me but sounds different.
But now I'm back
to visit both, and I need to point
to my first hotel room;
to the mortuary above which
my tall half-chinese half-german
punkrockboyfriend fingered me
like a book in his little bed;
and to the hospital where our bonemother
died so late or so early that
we were both sound asleep.

I didn't say it,
but: My sternum is breaking
with this, it's sinking
like Woodward as Detroit rises around
my brother's turn, rises and falls.
Falls not at all like this light summer rain
but hard, like someone else's memory,
insistent, unwanted, but suddenly,
and again, being claimed.

Palimpsest

After leaning at the bar
against the initials and devotions carved
by others, he now has the vague impression
we've met someplace before.

He's almost thinking he might
remember my name. He's thinking
of my eyes. He's thinking of reproducing,
transposing those lines on his palms
onto my waist. He's thinking I'm carved
of a sweet smelling wood. He's almost already
thinking of running into me again.

Me? I'm imitating myself. I'm walking
over to him. I'm talking, moving
my eyes. I'm branding a tattoo
of his heart wrapped in my name
under his sleeve.

He's thinking something like:
she's the only copy in existence.
He's imagining my footprints
in sand and in snow.

I'm cutting
into the thinly rolled dough
of his life. I'm making
over and over
the shape that is me.

He's thinking
my teeth are making marks
in his skin.

He thinks my skeleton a fossil
he'll find in his flesh.

He's thinking of lifting me in one
motion:

The me that is weighty
seven cities deep.

The River Twists Like Lake Shore Drive

Like that guy from Chicago
who wanted to know if the Kuskokwim
was fresh water or salt.
Like those sex-crazed fish, drunk on water,
racing into my taut taut net
strung out across the river.
Like their iridescent scales still littering
the river's floor.
The way they suck your skin,
the way they stick to you,
the way they know:
you were once a fish and now you're drunk on air because
that's how you feel,
that's how foreign:
this is the way
we will eat and sleep and talk.
Even *real people* play it.
Inuit Adam and Eve probably played it.
Alaska is not far enough.
Once my friends were pulling me under and I had to swim
for my life.
Once I looked good standing there.
No one could see the inside of my head.
Once I had a plan,
once I saw myself as more than myself,
as more than just a fish.
And just last week the chant of an Eskimo woman old and ugly
and fat with the world: you can always get another man . . .
you can always get another man . . .
The task of it,
what I loved was the physical task of it:
pulling in something whole and alive and glittering,
something weighty and silvery and slick.

Angels and Moths

If a man once loved you,
he's turned you into a moth.

That's how he'll remember
the flutter: that numinous,
that beating, that winged.

Angels and moths:
that's who men love.

But I don't recollect like that.
I don't think I ever loved
that gently. And I've never
flown toward a burning
house, hoping, maybe
my faith lay in that
single thing left,
in that smoldering filigree.
I never reminisce
a sorrow that delicately shaped.

But sometimes I feel someone remembering
me that way: translucent,
crazy, awake only at night.
He's regretting his fingertips
were not wide or soft enough.
He's mourning me now.
He's imagining me eating away
at someone else's light.

And that's perfect.
That's exactly how
he always wanted to love
me. My wings,
my hair-like antennae
hanging;
my frenulum
between his forefinger
and his thumb.

An Imaginative Study In Degradation

This poem begins in this corner,
where barely awake and naked
I stand at the top of the stairs,
a bas-relief against a book-encased wall,
and watch you leave for the day.

You may ask: how does the nude
fit into the contemporary setting?
And Cézanne thought apples
were the most difficult fruit.

Remember the year I stopped eating apples?
Remember the summer I kept bringing home
abandoned chairs? A lucid Vincent wrote
to his brother: I have tried
to express the terrible passions
of humanity by means of red and green.
His self-portrait now hangs in the Fogg.
Remember the summer I had to walk
to the Lake just to feel anything at all?

When I descend late in the afternoon
there's a blue plate of heart-
shaped cookies, there's an orange
on the kitchen counter. I notice a crack
in the seam of the ceiling, a spider
vein on the inside of my knee.
What a still still life!

The rest of the day is a slanted floorboard.
The rest of the day is the color of absinthe.
Note the personal and detached attitude.
Note the application of arbitrary color.
The tilted perspective.
This poem is all surface.
You may stand where you choose.
This poem has no vanishing point.

The Unhoused Heart

I was without lathe
Or hacksaw, I was

Not much at salvage:
Over the years a few soft planks

Of shittimwood and a large jar
Of bitten nails.

So I hired me a shipwright
No mere apprentice

For the sake of the vessel:
Not just sail, and not just boat.

Enlisted him to launch me into
Hardship. He unjointed

Booms, tore down my jury-
Rigging, brought down the flawed

Bowsprit, the soot-covered
Spanker and the rest of my patchwork

Sails. Oh, he was stern, not gaff-
Headed, he went on gut-feeling,

Feeding me hardtack: three square-
Rigged masts and a homemade

Keel. But I was no Spar. Nothing stuck
To these ribs. And now

All that is left is the tarred breastbone
Of a ponderous bird.

But I had agreed, had said
I would do anything

To weigh down the smoke
In my nostrils.

I remember having pled: *anything, anything,*
For my keelhauledheart.

It's Shaped Like A Fork

This house is a mess. Full
of solid notions
that keep turning into objects:
this simple sadness
that's shaped like a fork
and the vague fear that crusts
these dishes. I'm vacuuming
over this grass-like pain.
Emptying pockets for the wash:
such a burden: not just wrappers
but keys and mints, those sticky
and sorrow-coated stones.
And this larger grief
that always needs to be folded.

All day I've been chewing
on my own acrid gloom,
trying to put away
the things you keep carrying
home from work: the possessions
of children and women
and drunks, stolen or cheated,
the tasteless unhappiness
of others into jars labeled:
Heartbreak, Injustice,
Just-Plain-Bad-Fucking-Luck.

Buhrstone

Morning after morning

The awakening village howls
Like an insect
About to be dipped in amber.

I separate myself from the sky

But still carry the inevitable
Dream of your body
Covered in butterflies or in bees.

Here's a living blanket for your grave.

Here's who I've quietly become:
A slightly wilder version of you. Your hands
Knead the dough for my bread

And my husband's flesh, thick and smooth.
They wash my breasts and hips, they light
My cigarette, they crack my beer.

You've been dead too long.

Morning after morning
The heavy amber of you
Around my neck, inside the heels

Of my boots. I wear your gloves.
Your winter scarves, your winter hair,
And that heavy shearling coat.

Soon I will forget how to preserve you.

But for now I continue to dream daily,
Morning after morning: your body blooming
In yellow wings, thousands of butterflies alighting

And you just lie there.

Morning after morning
The orange grass keeps burning
Under the grey grey sky.

It Was A Coffin That Sang

My mother danced the czardas all night
she held up the edges
of her long red skirt, a poppy
in her teeth, its seeds
freckling her white
white face. And what a Gypsy
God was: stamping his boots
and tying his scarves
across one eye, like a lunatic crazed
by what he had set going:
each wild drunk
dancer, the heel-to-toe
of each reckless life.

All night death was just a dance
she could rise to.
It was a coffin that sang

a rough Russian melody:

the world will end
and the world will end
and the world will end on
some bright morning.

I suffered
a terrible hangover
of faith.

Now I'm tired, and my mother is stiff
with the idea of bending, but she makes
one last extravagant gesture:

a throwing up of the arms.

Saxifrage and Cinquefoil

the fields and fields
of lowly lupine
have already slipped

your mind
as you carry the small
but heavy field guide
of your heart up
into the arctic meadows

the bogs and the marshes and the first clearing:

you have left a bare lightbulb burning in the small closet of your life
and your apartment burns, caves in on itself

keep walking

through the twisted roots of trees
and past the affectations of small animals:

what does it matter, who your brother marries?

ascend slowly

to where each death in your family covers over in saxifrage
and cinquefoil;

to where each life covers in the oblate leaves of forgetfulness and ascent

yes, here are the bog violets and the twin flowers
but you can no longer identify the small feeling inside you

and in fact there is a new grass sprouting
from your newly buried father's mouth

and your mother, your mother
is eternally elsewhere: a heavenly spray
of poppies

cornflowers

in a small field of rye . . .

and then the third plover
in which nothing opens but the long grass lays itself down

in the shape of a body you once
had the opportunity to love but turned down,

and why did you do that? haven't you
classified these simple things
before? you had already figured out
what was important to you,

didn't you?

but you can no longer divide your thoughts into layers,
and the flowers now come in waves

a billow of the palest pink

and something is choking you:
there is a delicate pollen in your long long throat

have you ever loved anything more?

(there was once a room in a house that filled in orange light)

have you ever loved anything?

more than this elusive something afloat
in the thin thin air?

didn't you once have a sister
who is now like my sister, a petal thin Lament?

and didn't you ask for this?
haven't you always been a sucker
for the personification of the heart? and

the soul? haven't you repeatedly addressed her?

what say you?

this is no longer your demesne?

surely, you did not have to climb this far
or meet anyone along the way to know this:

you could have stayed in your wall papered room
and seen it:

the dense dense heart
the soul both obligated and obliged

no, not flowering

as this is not your field, I will warn you:
the wild celery will turn out to be poisonous

even at this stunning altitude
we will prove ourselves

selfish and unkind

Klage

past, Mr. Roethke, past the unbearably beautiful fences, past the high-
strung clotheslines, past the clean white rectangular souls—no, not flap-
ping, it was a starched day, windless, the spinning all inside: in the brittle
spokes of bicycle wheels and in that one boy's singular face: the way the
eyes were smeared in, darkly, over the acute angles of rooftops, over the flu-
orescent moss down the narrow steps and down that soft slope of a moun-
tainside, through its red hair, yes, nearby the too tender buds of willows
and alongside the brook, just now regaining the use of its watery tongue,
over the stones that are birdeggs and the birdeggs that are stones——

until here you are: small and fallen
silent at the bottom of a spring day

and you have not even begun to contemplate death

and to top the night off
someone begins hammering
another kind of Lament
into a piece of wood

in a brightly lit basement
late on an almost purple spring
night so ripe in its own ache
it too starts to break
open:

in a lambent monody
of streetlights
and stars

Your TV Lit You Like A Roman Candle

that's not spring exploding

that's just the preacher's fat wife abloom
in a house dress covered in daisies and thick
weeds, her stout calves bare, sprouting
from the stumps of her ankle high boots

those aren't the sparks of fireworks

that isn't fireweed

that's just someone thawing
somebody else's life with a blowtorch

that's just the sun shortcircuiting the thin wiring of the trees
setting the night flaring

and the neighbor's house
spilling out its windows
the tv burning, turning the snow blue

lighting the old stove on the porch, licking
the burst brown recliner
into cerulean flame

you have turned the sound way way down

you have waited all winter
for someone to come out and lean back
into this life, face the detonating
sky

The Gauze Of Flowers, A Love Poem

Remember when we couldn't name it
because it was a meadow
wild with tulips, both bright
as snow and dull as fire?
Driving in circles to find
the right spot for our love, then
using a chair? My heart was still
an artichoke, layered and prickly.
But you kept making me nest my face
in that one thick bouquet.

And just this morning my love
was briefly stuck in my throat
as I remembered all the soil
and sadness, remembered seeing you
on certain streets and corners, remembered
all the rubble and the clang. Remember

how it is and isn't fragile?
How it speaks in ears and fingers
takes days and hours and still
it wants nothing and it wants more?

And just this morning
the flowers you brought home drank
in the sunrise, they fleshed themselves out
the way people do, shaking
the cold from their collars
as they move toward the fire,
rubbing together their hands, kindling
it back. Some days

we want our love to be fleshly.
But some days it's transparent.
It's like gauze.

It is and isn't fragile.

I dare you to name it.
I dare you to remember
the rubble and clang.

Bitterns, Heronries

It's not about how mottled or how distilled,
or how we were all wading,
yes, like birds, but toward what?

A toast to the bride.

Soon she will be weightless,
lifted like a glass. Soon she will be seen to
and through. A toast to the bride
for she's about to dehisce:

in a quiet house seven years later she snaps
on a light at three thirty in the dark
afternoon because the mountain has chosen
to marry the stars.

in a quiet house seven years later she knows
of what she speaks:

This was meant to celebrate love.
This tried hard to remember the way
he whispered, quietly, in my ear,
tried hard to forget that the deep booming cry
belongs only to the male, that he's a cross
between buzzard and bull.

This was the glass.
This was its lifting.
This was meant to celebrate
the mating of birds.

In Defense Of Marriage

Marry the black horse stuck
Dumb in her humble corral.

Marry the white fences; marry the fenceless
Moon and the defenceless sky.

Marry the feedlot and the threshing
Floor. Like the northern heaven to the southern

Stars, marry the kitchen table, its three strong
Legs. Marry the gate and the small intricate

Cuts on the key and the view spreading
Outback. The streetlamp

Weds the morning light, like that, take the
Nomad. Promise to forsake. Give in

To the cistern full of asters.
To the way the beloved

Story goes: *her body from a bone.*
And her soul out of nothing.

In a slowly spoiling month find out
You have married the house worn

Blue on the yellowing hill: each of its
Slow budding bedrooms. Marry one or two

Or three varieties of light, in three or four
Different *lifetimes*. I meant, *windows*.

Mate, be forsaken.

I married the way moths marry.
I married hard.

Ovarian Tree

All night the dull ache
of an overripe dream: a room
swollen with women—Look
at their hands, their hair, fern-like,
falling—
bouquets of adder's tongue
hung by the root—
falling
in a gravity that rests so low
it drags on my heart, bends
down on these boughs; the hysteria
of hands and hair and gravity
and a beauty so rare
it is familiar: Look
at their waists, that's how they bend.
Look at their wounds, that's where
their children play. They fall
from my life until
there are no women left,
only children pulling at berries, and berries dropping
and dreaming of a new blossoming.

When I'm awake, I'll call this curvature of the soul a state.
When I'm awake, (where are the women?)
I will have forgotten.

This Is The Way I Carry Mine

Four hours' sleep tucked
behind my eyelids and this small city
starts interrogating me
under a stream of thick morning light:
As if you had any business shaking
the hands of the insane.
As if you were doing somebody
a favor.

Last night I knew what I could tell it,
I could defend myself, but this morning,
this morning it's hard to tell
if what's melting is the snow
or the trees. Around the corner,

inside the White Spot,
the cigarette machine glows
like it's midnight, like it's midnight *again*
and I still don't know what to say
to the unaffected, to the trusting
drunks, to the women who have lost their waists
but nevertheless stick their feet
into strappy sandals, who hang earrings
as if they were hanging light.
Have you seen the pure white rage
of the sky?

I don't know what to call out
to the pool players: to the thin-men, wide-eyed,
and I don't know how to address the simple-hearted
bartender: Excuse me, sir

as far as I can see we're calling this day
a wash.

It's morning and the city demands to see
the way we will carry ourselves
into the new light. The city insists
on receiving our dignity.
The city expects to hear our beautiful stutter.

It's time to go. Time to tuck the night
lovingly, like a skateboard, under the crook
of our childlike arms.

Outside, the thin line left in the sky
is exhausting itself.

Silkweed

the bride in a pale peach cocoon
spun by the tender mouth
of an insect

the young broom, a tufted ear of corn,
thinking of mouths emptying
so he can enter

This Cold Way Of Life

summer was
a tenderness
as transparent
and simple

as the word
blouse

as fragile as
poppies

steadying
their hearts
in the heavy wind

the wildflowers
have sown themselves
into the shape
of a grave

the garden
overgrown
and our awe

that old kitchen chair
left to winter
under the stars

the lean-to of those
few warm days
is flapping

and the tide is pulling
open
our mouths

A Seasonal Dwelling

The thinking soul is conducting an experiment. The method
of investigation: as soon as you have felt something,

throw it away.

She has discarded several
large cities. There are porches
she refuses to return to.

Rivers and dresses
already seen-through.

Rows of almond trees.
Bridges.

She has never seen the Southern Plains.
Has never dived for memories into a swimming hole
or an ocean. Tomorrow night she hopes
to be lifted once again by painfully clear sky.

 To be disappointed once again by aurora borealis.

Welcome To Lascaux

What I'd like to suggest
are chimney swifts and charm quarks
pinochets, jaruzelskis,
the upanishads.

What seeped into the cave of your brain
while you weren't looking?

What did they manage to sketch on the walls, drop
on the floor: the street
art, the railroad ties, the graffiti: FUCK YOU
and the way you always want
to lay something down.

What I have decided is to choose
to remember only the good things:

the way he used a blowtorch
as a means of prayer, the way isinglass
is an adhesive, an agent
that clarifies. The way she told time
by checking a mirror, then checking
on her arms.

She Was Just A Sketch

 a thin girl under a thick sky

so thin, each rib stood
for something

something to which this great tenderness,
a mere irrational love
toward certain flowers
and trees,
could attach

I've Always Been One To Delight
In The Misfortunes Of Others

Just the garlic rotting in the cupboard under the disconnected phone
and a letter from St. Louis: *Koh-I-Noor*
(the Pakistani restaurant where I now work)
is like a church. During the day I am still
dedicated to the life long study of schizophrenia, I read
all about it and it makes me cry. Dear Lord,
I pray, lick my plate clean.
and a postcard: *Memphis is just like Detroit!*
I feel right at home at Graceland!
and two pages of Czech serifs from a typewriter on a kitchen table in
    Prague.
The voice they sound speaks Ukrainian: *Olenko!*
If only my hands would stop shaking I could write you in person.
We were idealistic, we are a little disappointed, my new grandson is two.

Like Kerosene

Yes, it's daily
that we move into each other—but this morning
I was separate even from myself—
my hands were shovels, I had mosquito netting for hair,
and the insect beating against the night
was my heart. My name was hollow
and the sky was made of shale when

I walked into a part of morning
I've never seen: the sky still heavy, still
smoldering with the nighttimes of others,
the drunkenness and sorrow rising like dew, like fog,
like smoke back into the clouds. Suddenly,
my face was wet with it. I wanted to lie down
with it. To rest against the almost exhausted night.

Uncertain of what to do there
I started dividing the layers, the sediment,
thinking: Usually, I sleep through his sadness.

And the morning asking: Why do you keep track
of the middle of the day when you should be
waxing the moon? How can these young fragile branches
be left out in the darkness, and who set that darkness
wandering inside your heart? Who can your love ignite,
like this, like kerosene?

And then the sky lit the morning.
And then I went in to set my own house on fire.
And then I lay down next to you:
a body filling with feathers or with snow
asking: and who are you that my love can light
like this, like kerosene.

The Silt Of Sleep

Men begin to look like horses,
children like puppets
and a flat-stomached tree-girl
is welcoming back
the well-traveled birds:
red-throated, green-winged,
yellow-breasted and black. Sleep
climbs down off my shoulders,
a monkey wrapping its tail
around nothing but air. I dream
of snow-covered fronds,
a not quite frozen river, a tundra swan.
I dream a tale
of loneliness and alienation
as you pull up the knees
of your own sleep. I dream ice
rotting. Falling through
I dream a circling luna-moth.
I dream the string that holds
a papier-mâché solar system
near a window. I dream
the flutter of a light
green. I dream the children
who are puppets and the men
who are horses and the flat-stomached
tree-girl who might be standing
in for me, as your heart beats,
once for the you who is sleeping,
once for the you who runs
in the dream. Dream
a long procession of people.
Dream no weeping,
but so many sighs. Dream of butchers,
dream grave-diggers. Dream outcasts.
I dream the shape
of your lips, of the vowels

in your throat as you twitch
with the idea of setting
me on fire. Of lifting this
huge weighty carpet
from the wire-framed earth.
Of stepping out of this garment of flesh.
Dream that mustard seed.
Dream the undone
rising, wet, from their graves.
Tearing through
the silt of sleep.
A ceremony.
An apostasy.
Dream the V of flight.
Dream arctic tern,
dream snow-goose,
dream old-squaw.

Dream the sadness
that sleep will deposit.

Logical Games For The Unbeliever

All night I kept solving for G.
Now, through this dark morning,
the equation escapes
at the sad speed of light.

There are so many things I don't understand. The future
comes and it's no longer excited
to be here.

There are so many things I can't know. My old friends,
are they happy?

That small square of light

I went and sat inside it
and my heart lifted,
I swear it.

All The Natural Movements Of The Soul

the swan dive
the back flip
the jack knife

the way it wants to lean over things—

I was bent over my poems
like some crazy mother. Dinner was burning
on the floor. Yes, the distinct smell
of piss. Not much washing
but the spinning, the rinsing,
the sad steam of those who launder hung
in the air; there were slots for quarters,
they were the sockets of my eyes.

I don't want to blame anyone, but somehow:

the situation is always grave.

Then one afternoon, everything goes into remission.

Then there are whole days when nothing happens,
when I start asking simple questions like:

in what do you believe?

The way the soul wants
to lean over things,
the way the soul wants to leave

the way it wants to write
another lunch poem
it wants to protect itself
it wants to become famous
at the same time.

There were whole day-long days,
summer days like grace notes:

the trill of being high on a porch
that wrapped itself around the stars.

We sat around trying to name
the things that do not exist.
We sat there wanting to touch
everything again and again, only this time
we would be blindfolded, our arms ribboned
behind our backs, using only our tongues.

I thought: please don't grow
familiar. I think I said it out loud:
Please don't let me love you
that horrible way.

The situation is grave:

the way we lean over each other, the way years
later we emerge: hunchbacked, hooded,
with full grown tender things called souls.

Perhaps By Then You Will No Longer Be In Love

Although you have betrayed him in a dream,
you have betrayed him, and the infidelities
of sleep will change you: you

will find yourself suddenly in love
with the two young women
outside your window
whose voices and laughter fell

groundward

with last winter's snow. You will begin to think:
I am beginning to move among them.
But only you will be wearing a snap-brimmed
hat. When the knock comes, it will knock

a certain reticence. It will leave
your door covered in white-knuckles.

And the windows will no longer breathe, they will die

like paintings. And you will no longer be
worrying the stars into meaning, they will
already mean something, but that will only be the wind,
only the wind that will be

keen and keening.

All else will remain hidden and nameless.
By which I mean: *your soul*. By which I mean

you will begin by missing

your old sadness, that old country: a country
fielded in rye. And a strange sore
will just then start to form
underneath your tongue.

You will always find yourself being unfaithful to someone.

You will always be gathering something from the landscape
without poems:

then, finally, winter,
to once again
thin things out, down

to those two women's
voices. *And their laughter, their laughter falling
with the new snow?*

Perhaps by then you will no longer be in love.

Your infidelities will have changed you.

The Eccentric Practices
Of Certain Medieval Saints

I am heavy when I return to you
but it's a heaviness made
of neither gravity nor grace.

Should One Prefer Purity To Intensity Of Soul?

While you are gone, I keep the house
quiet. Did I ever tell you,

I once heard a woman speak of her loneliness
as if it were a small bird. Imagine: her sorrow

had a wingspan! A screaming saw

tearing through the soundless space
of this late summer day. And then, the beginnings

of rain. I sit here, follow a schoolgirl
walking home to undress her uniform sadness:

a grey plaid kilt. The gentle faced dog next door
at her picture window: it's not so much

the view that has affected her thinking
as the stubborn way the glass seems able to hold it.

She has a soul as thick as steak. That's her master's
misery spreading like red geranium against the dark blue house

the light blue sky filling with the confetti of birds.
Perhaps longing is just the heart changing

its colors. I noticed you barely saw me this morning
as I, barechested, ate my soft-boiled egg.

And all day I have wanted to ask you . . .

Quiet afternoon, the thick red thatch covering
in a fine netting of fluorescent moss, and then the rain

beginning to end. Don't worry. By the time you get here
the window will be wide open.

I will be naked, sound, asleep.

Sleep Was An Inlet

as well as a falling
into and out of the meadow
we passed earlier that afternoon.
The skunk cabbage a shade of yellow
that urged me to remember
how happy I was, or resolved to be, simply
because I had found myself standing
in a ley of misnamed yellow
calla lilies thinking: That's surely the shape
of the heart: open yet twisting
something strange, not at all delicate
at its core. Sleep was an inlet

as well as a folding
back around the fire. We had set
that whole week burning,
my brother saying something in an even voice
about his other life, the daily one,
the one he would have to recede to: the strangers,
the buildings, the hassle, as if only the mountain
had a face he could trust. You nodded.
I watched you nod at Oliver's Inlet
as if you were nodding toward
some other way of life. Sleep was an inlet as well

as a rising back
into the chair I had pushed
away from my desk. I kept getting up
to feed words to the fire:
heart. spathe. spadix. A book kept opening
to that same page. You came home kissing me
on the forehead with Hegel's lament: *only one man*
I know understands me, and even he does not.
I kept restoring that piece
of sky. The geese mating, mating.
The brown bears and the black-tailed

deer resolving, resolving
once again, to live in peace.

I kept leaving the mountainside
I was tucked into.

I was dreaming in sentences
declarative and short.

The yellow place I had left.

The yellow place I had left off
living, I kept returning to mark.

Around The Edges Of A Cold Cold Day

Under the ice they're dragging the river,
but I don't mean for this to signify
some kind of casualty, some kind of loss.
Even now a bicycle is being stubbornly
pedaled around the edges
of this wintry day, the cold
snapping in its spokes, the red metal frame.
Hitting everyone in the face,
the fevered sun wants things
to be louder, a little something
in exchange for the patina, a little
something for all this gloss.

But just the breath of the figure
floating above the bicycle,
and that clump of warmth
I think I'll call his heart, pumping
petals wrapped in a fluorescent wreath
of thorns, is just the evaporation of loss.

This day feels like it'll crack,
the ice will surely part and unveil
the flushed body of the guy
you heard of on the radio, finally
found, hunting underwater caribou
all these months; his wife still sweeping
the river with the hook of her mind.

Funny how the river lived.
Funny how my life continued.
All the glaring stories I walked over
as I collected my mail by way of the frozen
slough. They seemed solid as ice.
But how expertly I must have swum
through this prolonged winter, how deftly

I must have navigated this cold body
of water, not to have lost the feeling
in my fingers, this feeling in my lungs.

As Empty As A Church, I Believe I Am A Small Testament To The Failing Relationship Between Space And Light

The progress, if any, could not be called spiritual.

Those were days made entirely of dusk.
Those were days that wasted themselves.

So I would walk it there, a soul wanting to take a small mountain side
for its body.

The doors were thick, but I could hear them,
quietly screaming about love.

Walk, until I could see it: a light
full of small holes, quivering
as if leafed, but with no suffering inside it.
Walk, until that small mountain
would flicker inside me.

But the day would go on, steadily aching
in its own endless twilight, evenly humming
the darkening light.

Until finally, someone turned on the night's first noisy star.

Then, someone lit another.

They would warm themselves against that cold blue light.

But I would wait, let the room deepen around me, let the children
with their thick notebooks carry home
the spiraling night.

Until, it was moving in slow motion.
Until, it was a dizzy gull,
the word *inland* hanging from its beak
like a thick black snail.

Until I was sure God had failed me. In my unlit room,
in that daylong dusk I had not even managed
to memorize the side of someone's yellow house,

the three good scars that were its windows.

Postcard

Lately, I am capable only of small things.

Is it enough
to feel the heart swimming?

Jim is fine. Our first
garden is thick with spinach
and white radish. Strangely,
it is summer

but also winter and fall.

In response to your asking:
I fill the hours,
then lick them shut.

Today, not a single word, but the birds
quietly nodding
as if someone had suggested
moving on.

What was that perfect thing
some one who once believed in god said?

Please, don't misunderstand:
We still suffer, but we are
happy.

Against Devotion

It's just the same old raving
condolence. The same old wild sympathy
pulled up to prove you're not
without a heart. The fevered understanding
offered from the barstool, from this side
of the confessional's grate. The ardent
I'm-so-sorry, the willing *I-hear-you*,
as the gentle samaritan you are
inconspicuously leans away from the crazed
whisper: *My life's so fucked-up.*
It's just someone else's violent
dying. It's just your childhood friends stuck
in an oversized world. The crippled
talking. The exhausting
confiding. The not really
caring. It's the simple fact that
what's most touching
is the angle at which some old roof leans
against the sky. The shockingly thin
trees, the stunning mosaic
of light. The way the stars keep
arranging themselves
into constellations. The way the moon's
always somewhere
in the sky. What's most heartbreaking
is this rib piercing this lung. That I'm
as breathless as this
over nothing. Wanting everything
bending, layered and resilient: the parquetry,
the click of heels like the stove
setting itself on fire: My friends,
it's our hearts, we should be
walking around grabbing our hearts,
for what could be more burdened,
more efflorescent? Tell me, what's
as unfolding, as spiked and as shooted
as this, our dissilient heart.

This Specific Tree

You know you have walked toward it
but it arrives at you.
Through wild rose and a row of chokeberry—
each translucent pellet a word
gathered, but not yet understood—
stands the loosely framed clearing
and this specific tree.

The compass needle
does not come to rest in your hands,
it points in awkward directions,
mimicking the positions of your arms and legs,
toward caliginous memories. It indicates
the baldness of death and the length
of forgetting. These are your bearings.

That's how it will always be
held. You cross a field
of cottonwood or ascend an incline
of newly laid snow and unexpectedly
it finds you.

Once there, rest
against the tipped root of the giant cedar
and remember arriving here
the last time, and then,
the time before that.

There May Be More Of This World
Than Can Possibly Exist

Not just the cosmos you have thickly sown into the small field
just east of your heart, but all that is held
in disbelief, in unfaith. Not only the barbed paragraphs of scrub
willows or the thoughts as thin as telephone wires,
but what's left of the salt lick of your soul,
or of the woman you married.

And what isn't: that half-built house, laid bare and open,
forsaken by the suicidal bricklayer, the carpenter's deconstructing
hands. The winged mail carrier, just now
rounding the corner, feeling depressed again,
praying for deliverance or rain. No, not just that.
Not only the Dostoyevsky reeling
in his walkman: but everything the brothers did, thought about
doing, said . . .

And all that is held so high.
And all that is swimming, way underneath it.

Not just the trajectory, not only the first stone
or the second, but what's left in your wrist, that which is
ancient, the african village that dances inside you, the medicine
you are feeding and the whole sky. The sky that's no longer refusing

the ground and the heretics, the martyrs; the skeptics now willing
to take certain things under consideration:
the god that exists, and the one that doesn't.

Not just the determination of the stars, but the stars
newly determined to understanding the clear
clear night. The blind appetite
of the senses, so well fed, it's dreaming of vinegar
and malt. And everything else
you can't, as luck will have it, bring yourself
to consider: the white-tailed deer stepping gently

out of the scratchy thicket,
her soft warm tongue, sweet and fresh as milk.

And all those quiet hours when you thought you knew
what you were talking about,
but were only scrubbing your soul with salt,
saying: let what is grain turn to grain,

just not meaning it.